HAL•LEONARD
INSTRUMENTAL
PLAY-ALONG

AUDIO
ACCESS
INCLUDED

PLAYBACK+
Speed • Pitch • Balance • Loop

# VIOLIN

T0071600

Audio arrangements by Peter Deneff

To access audio visit:
**www.halleonard.com/mylibrary**

Enter Code
4371-5518-8868-5028

ISBN 978-1-70516-361-0

HAL•LEONARD®

Visit Hal Leonard Online at
**www.halleonard.com**

Contact us:
**Hal Leonard**
7777 West Bluemound Road
Milwaukee, WI 53213
Email: info@halleonard.com

In Europe, contact:
**Hal Leonard Europe Limited**
42 Wigmore Street
Marylebone, London, W1U 2RN
Email: info@halleonardeurope.com

In Australia, contact:
**Hal Leonard Australia Pty. Ltd.**
4 Lentara Court
Cheltenham, Victoria, 3192 Australia
Email: info@halleonard.com.au

# ALL OF YOU

VIOLIN

Music and Lyrics by
LIN-MANUEL MIRANDA

# COLOMBIA, MI ENCANTO

VIOLIN

Music and Lyrics by
LIN-MANUEL MIRANDA

# THE FAMILY MADRIGAL

VIOLIN

Music and Lyrics by
LIN-MANUEL MIRANDA

# DOS ORUGUITAS

VIOLIN

Music and Lyrics by
LIN-MANUEL MIRANDA

# SURFACE PRESSURE

VIOLIN

Music and Lyrics by
LIN-MANUEL MIRANDA

9

# WAITING ON A MIRACLE

VIOLIN

Music and Lyrics by
LIN-MANUEL MIRANDA

rit.

# WE DON'T TALK ABOUT BRUNO

VIOLIN

Music and Lyrics by
LIN-MANUEL MIRANDA

13

# WHAT ELSE CAN I DO?

VIOLIN

Music and Lyrics by
LIN-MANUEL MIRANDA